DEADLY AND INCREDIBLE ANIMALS

TOP 10 Marine Animals

Jay Dale

MACMILLAN

LIBRARY

First published in 2011 by
MACMILLAN EDUCATION AUSTRALIA PTY LTD
15–19 Claremont Street, South Yarra 3141

Visit our website at www.macmillan.com.au or go directly to
www.macmillanlibrary.com.au

Associated companies and representatives throughout the world.

National Library of Australia
Cataloguing-in-Publication data

Dale, Jay.
   Top ten marine animals / Jay Dale.
   ISBN: 9781 4202 8248 1 (hbk.)
   Dale, Jay. Deadly and incredible animals.
   Includes index.
   For primary school age.
   Marine animals – Juvenile literature.
591.77

Publisher: Carmel Heron
Commissioning Editor: Niki Horin
Managing Editor: Vanessa Lanaway
Proofreader: Georgina Garner
Designer: Cristina Neri, Canary Graphic Design
Page layout: Peter Shaw, Julie Thompson and Cristina Neri
Photo researcher: Legendimages
Illustrators: Andrew Craig and Nives Porcellato
Production Controller: Vanessa Johnson

Printed in China

Acknowledgements
The author and publisher are grateful to the following for permission to reproduce
copyright material:

Front cover photograph: Great White Shark (Carcharodon carcharias) courtesy of Getty Images/
Armin Maywald/Foto Natura.

Photographs courtesy of: age fotostock/Reinhard Dirscherl, **8**, **24**; ANTPhoto.com.au/Tom
Campbell/SpecialistStock/Aurora Photos, **21**; AUSCAPE/Frank Woerle, **25**; Australian Red
Cross, **30**; Dreamstime.com/Anankkml, **6** (crocodile), /Crisod, **6** (stonefish), /Cynoclub, **6**
(lionfish), /Desertdiver, **11**, /Naluphoto, **6** (tiger shark), /Sullivan, **10**, /Willtu, **6** (great white
shark), /Yobro10, **6** (stingray), **12** (top); Getty Images/Gary Bell, **28**, /Jeff Rotman, **15**, /Paul
Sutherland, **29**; iStockphoto/Chris Dascher, **18**, /zennie, **12** (bottom); marinethemes.com/Kelvin
Aitken, **23**, **26**; naturepl.com/Doug Perrine, **17**; NOAA Sea Grant Program, Photo Collection
of Dr. James P. McVey, **27**; Photolibrary/Alamy/Peter Arnold, Inc., **13**, /Alamy/Martin Harvey, **6**
(cone snail), /Alamy/Poelzer Wolfgang, **14**, /Reinhard Dirscherl, **3**, /Keith Gillett, **6** (jellyfish), /
Karen Gowlett-Holmes, **5**, /Yves Lefèvre, **20**, /L Newman & A Flowers, **6** (octopus), back cover,
/OSF/Chris and Monique Fallows, **4**, **19**, /Jeffrey L. Rotman, **6** (sea snake); Shutterstock/
Galushko Sergey, **7** (background), **12** (background), **18** (background), **22** (background), /Teguh
Tirtaputra, **22**, /Undersea Discoveries, **16**. Stingray silhouette with 'That's incredible!' feature
© Shutterstock/gaga, **7**, **8**, **10**, **12**, **14**, **16**, **18**, **20**, **22**, **24**, **26**, **28**.

While every care has been taken to trace and acknowledge copyright, the publisher tenders their
apologies for any accidental infringement where copyright has proved untraceable. They would
be pleased to come to a suitable arrangement with the rightful owner in each case.

The publisher would like to thank the Australian Red Cross for their help reviewing the first aid
advice in this manuscript.

The author would like to thank Sharnika Blacker for helping with the research on this book.

Please note
At the time of printing, the Internet addresses appearing in this book were correct. Owing to
the dynamic nature of the Internet, however, we cannot guarantee that all these addresses will
remain correct.

CONTENTS

GLOSSARY WORDS
When a word is printed in **bold**, you can look up its meaning in the Glossary on page 31.

DEADLY AND INCREDIBLE ANIMALS

Many animals are deadly to other animals. They are deadly to their prey and sometimes even to their **predators**. Over many thousands of years, these animals have developed incredible behaviours and features to find food, to defend themselves from predators and to protect their young.

Deadly and incredible features and behaviours

Different types of animals have different deadly features and behaviours. Deadly and incredible features include strong jaws, razor-sharp teeth and stingers or fangs for injecting **venom** into prey. Deadly and incredible behaviours include stalking, hunting and distracting prey before attacking and killing it.

Animals such as lions use their incredible size and strength to smash, crush and rip apart their prey. Excellent eyesight helps many **nocturnal** animals hunt their prey under the cover of even the darkest night.

◄ A great white shark uses its size and strength to leap out of the water to catch a seal.

DEADLY AND INCREDIBLE MARINE ANIMALS

In the oceans and along the coastal shorelines live some of the world's most deadly and incredible animals.

What are marine animals?

Marine animals are a very diverse group of animals that live in oceans, seas, bays and **estuaries**. Marine animals include fish, reptiles, **molluscs** and **coelenterates** (say *si-len-tuh-rayts*).

IN THIS BOOK

In this book you will read about the top ten deadliest marine animals on Earth – from number 10 (least deadly) to number 1 (most deadly). There are many different opinions on which of the marine animals should top this list. The marine animals in this book have been selected based on their ability to either stalk and hunt down their prey, or kill with deadly venom or powerful jaws.

▶ Deadly and incredible marine animals come in all shapes and sizes.

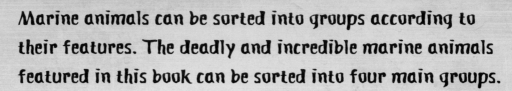

Marine animals can be sorted into groups according to their features. The deadly and incredible marine animals featured in this book can be sorted into four main groups.

Fish

Fish are **vertebrates**. Most have jaws, fins, scales, and gills for providing oxygen to the blood. Sharks and stingrays have a boneless skeleton made of a tough elastic material called cartilage. They are known as cartilaginous fish.

▼ lionfish, page 10

▲ stonefish, page 20

▲ stingray, page 12

▼ tiger shark, page 16

▲ great white shark, page 18

Marine reptiles

Marine reptiles are cold-blooded vertebrates. They have scales and live in warm waters.

▼ saltwater crocodile, page 24

▲ beaked sea snake, page 14

Molluscs

Molluscs are **invertebrates**. They have soft bodies, which are usually protected by a shell.

◄ blue-ringed octopus, page 22

◄ marbled cone snail, page 26

Coelenterates

Coelenterates are invertebrates. They have soft bodies, which are supported by the water they live in. They do not have a shell.

▶ box jellyfish, page 28

Features for survival

Deadly and incredible features and behaviours help marine animals to survive in their ocean and coastal **habitats**.

DEADLY FEATURES AND BEHAVIOURS

Feature	Behaviour / use of feature	Animal examples
powerful jaws and large razor-sharp teeth	grab, crush, hold and rip apart prey	tiger shark, great white shark, saltwater crocodile
strength and size	crush, hold and rip apart prey	great white shark, saltwater crocodile
spines	inject **venom** into prey	lionfish, stonefish
camouflage	hide from and stalk prey	lionfish, blue-ringed octopus, stonefish
stinger	inject venom into prey	box jellyfish
bite	inject venom into prey	beaked sea snake, blue-ringed octopus
barb or harpoon	inject venom into prey (barb can remain in victim)	stingray, marbled cone snail
speed of movement	catch prey	beaked sea snake, tiger shark, great white shark, marbled cone snail, lionfish
advanced senses	smell prey or, detect small movements and blood in water	tiger shark, great white shark

THREATS TO MARINE ANIMALS

Threats to marine animals and their **habitats** are increasing as the world's population increases and humans demand more goods and services.

Threats to survival

Many marine animals have become **extinct** and others are **endangered**. The saltwater crocodile is now wiped out in Burma (Myanmar), Thailand, Laos, Vietnam and Cambodia. Many whale **species**, such as the humpback and the fin whales are endangered and nearly extinct from **overfishing**. The number of great white sharks has decreased by between 60 and 95 per cent in the last 50 years.

That's Incredible!

Scientists estimate that between 500 000 and 5 million marine species are yet to be discovered. Threats to marine environments mean many of these species may be destroyed before they are even seen by humans.

The saltwater crocodile has disappeared from many areas in Asia, but it is very common in northern Australia where it is protected from human threats.

Main threats to marine animals

The main threats to marine animals are human activities. Different methods of fishing can greatly reduce the numbers of many sea creatures.

THREATS TO MARINE ANIMALS

Threat	Explanation	Impact
Whaling	Whaling is illegal around the world. Some countries claim they hunt and kill whales for scientific research.	Too many whales are being killed and they cannot **breed** quickly enough to replace them.
Overfishing	Overfishing occurs when too many fish are caught each year. This means that the fish cannot breed quickly enough to replace the ones that have been caught.	Large populations of fish are being greatly reduced by overfishing in some parts of the world's oceans. Overfishing affects the whole of a **food chain**, leaving some animals without food.
Factory fishing	Large factory ships use modern equipment to suck up entire schools of fish from the water.	This fishing method does not leave any fish behind, which means there are no fish to breed and replace the fish that are caught. This can lead to **extinction**.
Bottom trawling	Large ships use huge nets with metal chains to trawl the bottom of the ocean.	This fishing method destroys marine **habitats**. It also kills other marine animals that the fishers do not want to catch.
Being caught as bycatch	Fishing nets not only scoop up schools of fish but also other marine life.	Every year, hundreds of thousands of marine animals, including whales and dolphins, are trapped in fishing nets and killed.
Pirate fishing	Modern-day pirates illegally take fish and other marine life from protected areas of oceans.	The fish and other marine life in the protected areas are in danger of becoming extinct.
Global warming	The warming of Earth is causing our oceans to heat up, too.	Warming of oceans causes changes to **ecosystems**. Many marine animals cannot survive these changes to their habitat.
Pollution	Many substances, such as sewage (waste from toilets) and chemicals from industrial and farming activities, get washed out into our oceans. Some rubbish from cities can also wash out into the ocean.	Chemicals and sewage cause damage to marine animals and ecosystems. Marine animals can get rubbish caught around their necks, feet, fins or flippers, which can kill them.

10

LIONFISH

The lionfish is beautiful but deadly. Its long and colourful spines are **venomous**. The lionfish's **aggressive** nature keeps even the largest ocean **predators** away.

venomous dorsal-fin spines

That's **Incredible!**

Lionfish are eaten as food in some parts of Asia. However, many more are sold and kept in home fish tanks.

eyes

There are many types of lionfish, and each one has its own unique pattern of zebra-like stripes.

fan-shaped pectoral fins

Deadly features: Usually 18 long, striped, needle-like spines containing **venom**

Predators: Grouper fish

Size: between 30 and 38 centimetres (12 to 15 inches) long

Lifespan: up to 15 years

Habitat: coral **reefs**, shallow coastal waters, near underwater caves and crevices

Distribution: ■

coastal areas in Indian and Pacific oceans, the north western coast of Australia, Indonesia, Papua New Guinea, Malaysia, the Philippines, some Polynesian islands, southern Japan, southern Korea and the eastern coast of the United States

Night-time hunter

The lionfish hunts mostly at night. During the day, it hovers quietly, **camouflaged** among coral reefs. The lionfish usually eats all that it needs in the first hour of darkness. As it closes in on its prey, it opens its mouth quickly, which causes the water to rush in. This is how the lionfish sucks its prey in. The prey get swallowed whole.

What's for dinner?
Lionfish eat small fish and shrimp.

Camouflage trickery

The lionfish's stripes are designed to trick other creatures in the ocean. The stripes make it difficult to work out how big the lionfish is, or even where it is! This allows the lionfish to sneak up on its prey.

▶ The lionfish sometimes spreads out its venomous spines and uses them to herd small fish into an area where they cannot escape.

STINGRAY

The stingray is not **aggressive**, but if it feels threatened, it may lash out with its poisonous barb and inject **venom** into its victim. It uses its jaw teeth to crush its prey.

The stingray's whip-like tail is armed with one or more poisonous barbs.

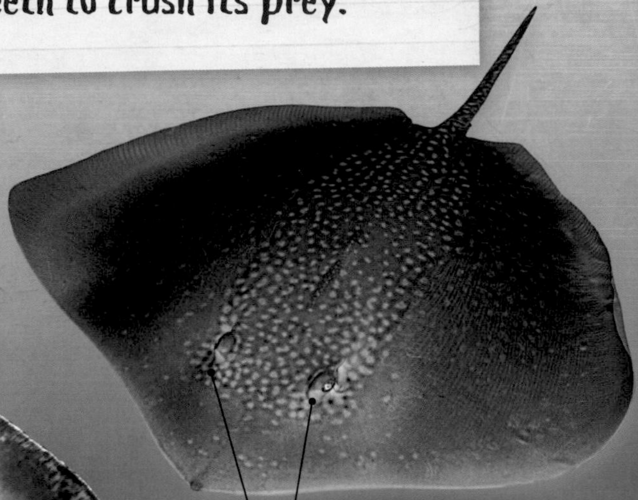

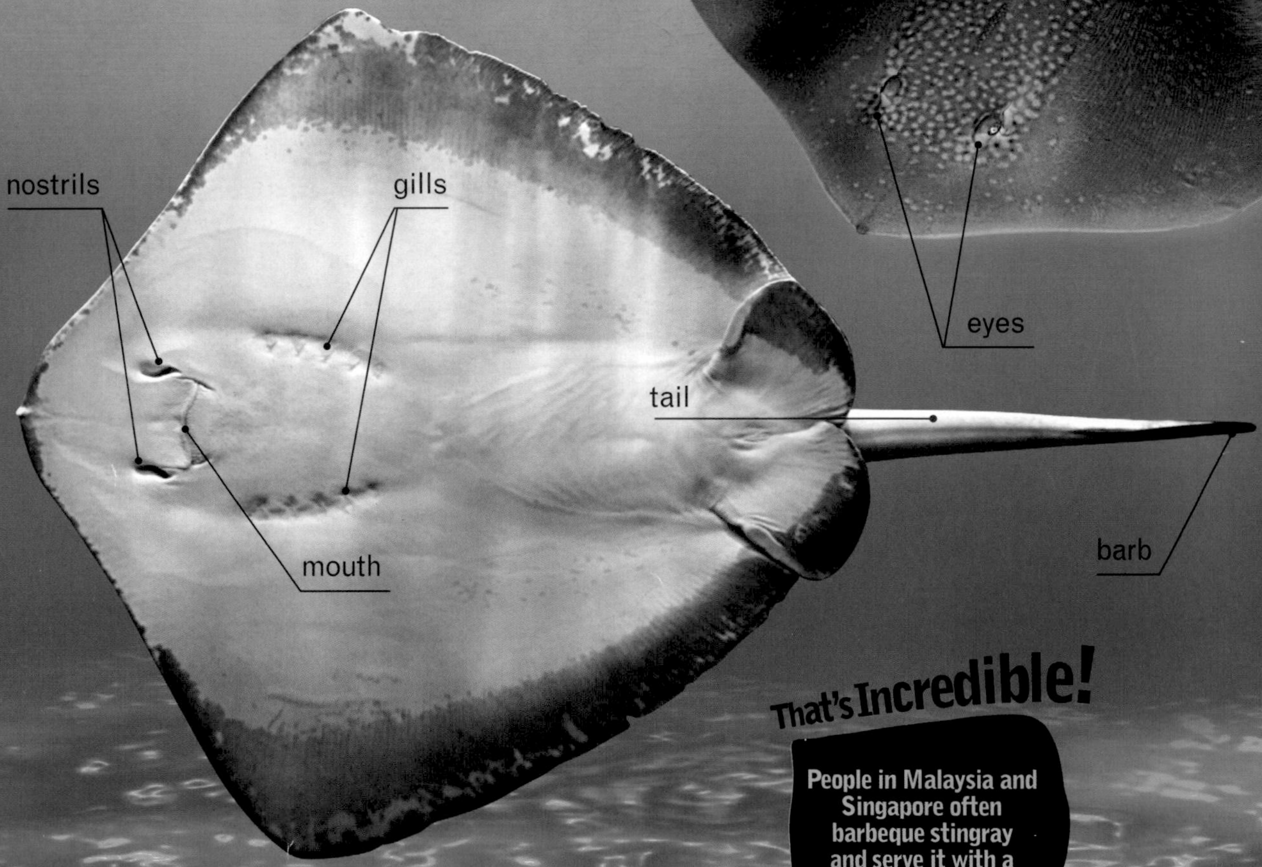

nostrils

gills

eyes

tail

mouth

barb

That's Incredible!

People in Malaysia and Singapore often barbeque stingray and serve it with a spicy sauce.

Deadly features: poisonous barb, crushing teeth

Predators: sharks, larger stingrays

Size: between 25 centimetres and 2 metres (10 in and 6.6 feet) long, including tail

Lifespan: 15 to 25 years

Habitat: shallow coastal waters

Distribution: temperate oceans worldwide

Hidden danger

The stingray is a shy creature that spends large amounts of time hidden on the ocean floor. Its sandy-grey colour and flat body allows it to **camouflage** itself and hide from **predators** – often only its eyes and tail can be seen. In this hidden position, it scans the ocean floor for food.

Crushing jaws

The stingray is related to the shark. It has powerful jaws, just like a shark. The stingray uses its strong jaws to crush prey, such as lobsters and crabs, which have hard external skeletons called exoskeletons.

What's for dinner?

Stingrays eat small fish, worms, crabs and **molluscs** such as clams, oysters and mussels.

▼ The stingray feeds along the ocean floor, using its jaw teeth to crush small sea creatures, such as crabs and clams.

BEAKED SEA SNAKE

Some experts believe the beaked sea snake has the deadliest **venom** of all snakes. One bite contains enough venom to kill more than 50 people.

That's Incredible!

A beaked sea snake has more young at one time than any other sea snake. Each litter averages about 18 live young, but sometimes there can be as many as 30!

paddle-like tail

eyes

The upper jaw of the beaked sea snake juts out over the lower jaw and looks just like a beak or a hook.

Deadly features: fangs for injecting venom are 2.5 to 4.5 millimetres (0.01 to 0.02 in) long

Predators: large fish and saltwater crocodiles

Size: between 60 and 150 centimetres (24 and 59 in) long

Lifespan: unknown

Habitat: shallow coastal waters with muddy or sandy bottoms, especially mud flats in **estuaries** and at river mouths

Distribution: ■
from the Persian Gulf region of the Indian Ocean (including coastal islands of India) to the Pacific Ocean (including the northern coast of Australia and many parts of South-East Asia)

Slithering hunter

The beaked sea snake uses its paddle-like tail to move through the water in search of prey. When it catches prey, it injects deadly venom into it using its fangs. The sea snake waits for the prey to become **paralysed** before eating it.

What's for dinner?
Beaked sea snakes eat catfish, puffer fish and eels.

Coming up for air

Like all reptiles, the beaked sea snake has to breathe air. It has nostrils on top of its snout. This allows it to keep most of its body under the water's surface while it breathes. The snake's nostrils close when it dives under the water.

Although the beaked sea snake comes to the surface to breathe air, it can remain under water for up to five hours.

TIGER SHARK

The tiger shark is a deadly and dangerous **predator**.
It has powerful jaws and razor-sharp teeth that can easily
slice through the flesh and bone of its prey.

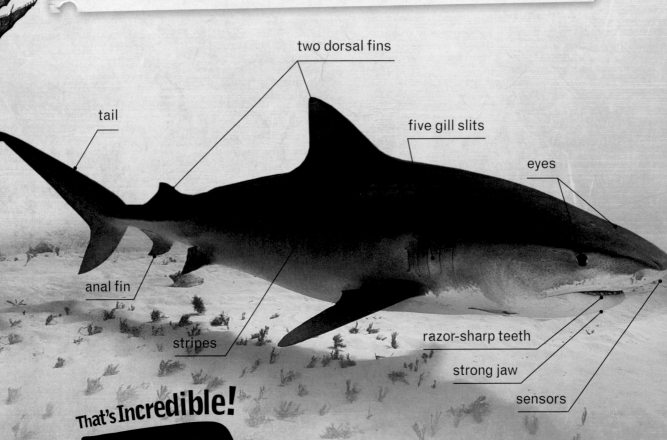

two dorsal fins

tail

five gill slits

eyes

anal fin

stripes

razor-sharp teeth

strong jaw

sensors

That's Incredible!

Tiger sharks are often called the 'garbage cans of the sea', because they are quick to eat anything that moves. Fishermen have found licence plates and old tyres in the stomachs of some tiger sharks.

A young tiger shark has tiger-like stripes on its back, which help **camouflage** it in shallow waters. These stripes fade when the shark gets older, like the one here.

Deadly features: razor-sharp teeth and strong jaws, excellent eyesight and smell, ability to sense small muscle movements of other animals

Predators: other tiger sharks and humans

Size: 3 to 6.5 metres (10 to 21 ft) long; weight 385 to 635 kilograms (849 to 1400 pounds)

Lifespan: up to 50 years

Habitat: deeper waters that line coral **reefs**

Distribution: ■
tropical and **temperate** oceans, mainly in coastal areas

Killer senses

The tiger shark has small sensors on the side of its upper body. These help it sense the muscle movements of other animals in the water. The tiger shark has an excellent ability to sense whether or not its prey is wounded.

A big appetite

The tiger shark eats all of its prey, and does not leave any pieces behind. It swallows small prey whole. When it eats large prey, it keeps biting it until it has eaten it all. Most tiger sharks spend most of their time hunting in deep waters on the edge of coastal reefs.

What's for dinner?

Tiger sharks eat anything that moves, including fish, seals, birds, smaller sharks, squids, turtles, stingrays, dugongs, sea snakes and dolphins.

▼ The tiger shark's wedge-shaped head and hooked tail allow it to move rapidly from side to side when chasing down prey.

GREAT WHITE SHARK

When a great white shark bites into its victim, it shakes its head from side to side, tearing off chunks of flesh with its teeth. It then swallows its prey whole.

The great white shark has rows of spare teeth that replace any teeth that may break off.

cone-shaped snout

five gill slits

dorsal fin

second dorsal fin

nostril   mouth

eye

pelvic fin

pectoral fin

triangular, serrated (saw-edged), razor-sharp teeth up to 7.5 centimetres (3 in) long

That's Incredible!

The largest great white shark caught was 6.4 metres (21 feet) long and weighed 3324 kilograms (7313 pounds). That's the same weight as an elephant!

Deadly features: size and weight, up to 3000 razor-sharp teeth

Predators: humans and killer whales

Size: average size 4.3 to 5.5 metres (14 to 18 ft), average weight 680 to 1800 kilograms (1499 to 3968 lb)

Lifespan: 30 to 100 years

Habitat: coastal surface waters in all major oceans, offshore waters of temperatures 12°–24° C (54°–75° F)

Distribution: ■
all major **temperate** and **tropical** regions in the world, most frequently found off southern Australia, South Africa, and the mid-western and north eastern coasts of the United States

Super senses

The great white shark cruises waters close to the coast, looking for prey. Like the tiger shark, the great white shark can sense even the smallest muscle movements in the water. It can smell even just one or two drops of blood in the water.

Surprise attack

The great white shark strikes very suddenly. It speeds up to attack its prey, often thrusting the prey out of the water as it breaks through the surface of the water. Sometimes a great white shark will take a large bite out of its prey and then wait for it to die.

What's for dinner?
Great white sharks eat dolphins, porpoises, seals, sea lions and dead whales.

The incredible speed of the great white shark's attack sometimes forces its prey out of the water.

STONEFISH

The stonefish is the deadliest fish in the world. Its spines contain poisonous **venom**, which can kill a human in two hours if untreated.

That's Incredible!

A stonefish can produce more than 1 million eggs, which stay inside the mother until they hatch. Only a few hatchlings survive in the open ocean, because most are eaten by other fish.

13 dorsal fins with spines

▼ When the stonefish is disturbed, it sticks up its poisonous dorsal-fin spines.

gills

tail

pectoral fin

Deadly features: 13 dorsal-fin spines that inject venom, **camouflage**, incredibly fast movement of spines

Predators: sharks and rays

Size: 30 to 50 centimetres (12 to 20 in) long

Lifespan: unknown

Habitat: coral **reefs** and shallow coastal waters

Distribution:
coastal areas in Indian and Pacific oceans, off the northern coast of Australia, Indonesia, Papua New Guinea, Malaysia, the Philippines, some Polynesian islands, southern Japan and southern Korea

Hidden danger

The stonefish is so well camouflaged that it looks like a lump of rock or coral. It can sit motionless for hours, waiting for prey to swim past. The stonefish's mouth points upwards, ready to suck in any creature that swims nearby. It swallows its prey whole.

What's for dinner?

Stonefish eat small fish, shrimp and other **crustaceans.**

Spiny defences

The stonefish uses its **venomous** spines to protect itself from **predators**. It is a slow-moving fish and would not be able to swim away from danger. It can raise its spines quickly to strike against predators. It does not use its spines to catch prey.

▼ The stonefish lies very still among the rocks, until it strikes with incredible speed and sucks in its prey.

21

BLUE-RINGED OCTOPUS

The blue-ringed octopus pounces on its unsuspecting prey, paralysing it with venom. This octopus then tears the prey apart and sucks out its flesh.

A large blue-ringed octopus can produce enough venom to kill ten adult humans.

That's Incredible!

The female blue-ringed octopus lays only one group of about 50 eggs. The eggs lie under her tentacles for nearly six months. She does not eat during this time and dies soon after the eggs hatch.

distinctive blue rings

head

tentacles

Deadly features: venom
Predators: whales, moray eels, birds and humans
Size: 5 to 20 centimetres (2 to 8 in) long
Lifespan: up to two years
Habitat: tidal rock pools

Distribution: ■
Pacific Ocean, from Japan to Australia

Warning colours

The blue-ringed octopus displays its warning colours to warn **predators** to leave it alone. When it is disturbed, it quickly changes colour, turning bright yellow with blue rings or lines.

Paralysing venom

The blue-ringed octopus uses its venom in one of two ways to catch its prey. It can squirt its **venomous** saliva into the water around its prey, paralysing it, or sometimes it will catch the prey in its tentacles and bite into it with its beak. The venom in its saliva paralyses the prey.

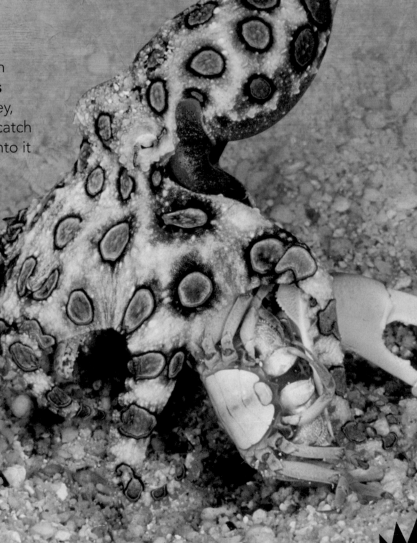

The blue-ringed octopus can use its long tentacles to trap its prey and its venom to paralyse it.

What's for dinner?
Blue-ringed octopuses eat small crabs, shrimp and fish (if they are fast enough to catch them).

23

3

SALTWATER CROCODILE

The saltwater crocodile is the world's largest reptile. It strikes with incredible speed, killing its prey with one snap of its powerful jaws.

That's Incredible!

A crocodile can hold its breath under water for up to one hour. To do this, it slows down its heart rate to two beats per minute.

large tail

65 teeth

▲ A saltwater crocodile uses its muscular tail to push itself through the water.

powerful jaws

Deadly features: powerful jaws, sharp teeth

Predators: Large crocodiles have no known **predators.** Younger, smaller crocodiles are prey for tigers and leopards.

Size: females 2 to 3.5 metres (6.6 to 11.5 ft) long, weight 120 to 250 kilograms (261 to 551 lb); males 4 to 6.5 metres (13 to 21 ft) long, weight 350 to 1000 kilograms (772 to 2205 lb)

Lifespan: 70 years

Habitat: freshwater swamps and rivers, **estuaries** and out at sea

Distribution: ■
South-East Asia, Australia, India, Papua New Guinea and Indonesia

The death roll

If a saltwater crocodile does not kill its prey with the first bite, it pulls its victim into a 'death roll'. The prey is rolled two or three times and then dragged under the water and drowned.

Powerful jaws

The saltwater crocodile has incredibly strong jaws, which allow it to inflict a vicious and crushing bite on its victims. Its jaws need to be strong to hold on to large prey as it drags the prey under water.

What's for dinner?

Young crocodiles eat insects, frogs, toads, **crustaceans**, small reptiles and fish. Older crocodiles eat small animals such as turtles, crustaceans, fish, small mammals and birds, as well as large animals such as water buffaloes.

▼ The saltwater crocodile bursts out of the water to snatch unsuspecting prey.

MARBLED CONE SNAIL

The venom of the marbled cone snail is one of the deadliest venoms on Earth. One drop is enough to kill 20 people. If a person was attacked by a marbled cone snail, they would most likely die within minutes, as there is no anti-venom.

radular opening (mouth)

That's Incredible!

The time it takes for the marbled cone snail to strike and suck a fish into its stomach is about 30 seconds.

The marbled cone snail's harpoon shoots out of its mouth like a torpedo. The harpoon can be shot in any direction, even backwards.

Deadly features: venomous harpoon, fast movement

Size: 14 to 16 centimetres (5.5 to 6 in) long

Lifespan: unknown

Habitat: warm and **tropical** coral **reefs**

Distribution: ■

reefs in Indian and Pacific oceans, around northern Australia, Indonesia, Papua New Guinea, Malaysia, southern Japan, southern Korea and along the south eastern coast of the United States

Harpoon hunter

The marbled cone snail attracts prey by waving its **proboscis** around like a worm. Less than a second after the prey touches the proboscis, the cone snail shoots a deadly harpoon from its mouth. The harpoon is coated in venom, which **paralyses** the creature in seconds.

What's for dinner?

Marbled cone snails eat marine worms, small fish, **molluscs** and other cone snails.

Eating prey whole

Once the prey is paralysed, the cone snail eats it whole. The snail has to come out of its shell to eat the prey. Without the protection of its shell, it may be attacked by **predators** while it is eating.

▼ A marbled cone snail uses a thread attached to its harpoon to suck prey back towards its shell.

27

BOX JELLYFISH

The box jellyfish (also known as the sea wasp) is one of the deadliest creatures on Earth. It has 60 tentacles, each with 5000 stinging cells that contain enough venom to kill 60 humans!

That's Incredible!

The box jellyfish tentacles are still deadly even when the jellyfish is dead or if the tentacles have been separated from its body.

manubrium (mouth)

tentacles

▶ The box jellyfish has four sides and is shaped like a cube or bell.

Deadly features: stinging cells in its tentacles with poisonous venom

Predators: butterfish, batfish, rabbitfish, crabs and turtles

Size: 20 centimetres (8 in) wide, tentacles 1 to 3 metres (3 .3 to 10 ft) long

Lifespan: less than one year

Habitat: close to shore when water is calm, near mouths of rivers, **estuaries** and creeks after rain

Distribution: ■
Indian and Pacific oceans, including north eastern to north western Australia, Indonesia, Papua New Guinea, the Philippines, southern and eastern Japan, coast of South-East Asia, eastern coast of India and Sri Lanka.

Instant death

The powerful venom of the box jellyfish stuns or kills its prey instantly. It then eats its prey whole through its large mouth, called its manubrium. The venom instantly stops the prey from struggling as it tries to escape. If the prey struggles, it could damage the box jellyfish's delicate tentacles.

Killer on the move

The box jellyfish hunts its prey by propelling itself through the water. Most jellyfish simply drift into their prey. The box jellyfish pumps water out of its bell-shaped body, which allows it to move itself through the water. It can even turn in the water, by pointing its body in a different direction.

▼ Inside each stinging cell is a thread coiled up, ready to shoot out and sting prey, such as this fish.

What's for dinner?
Box jellyfish eat small fish and **crustaceans**.

FIRST AID

Keep these first aid tips in mind if you are at the beach or swimming in **tropical** seas. Quick action can help reduce the impact of stings and bites from marine animals.

First aid when stung by a lionfish, stonefish or stingray

1 Soak the affected area in hot (not boiling) water.
2 If heat does not help, apply a wrapped cold pack. This will help relieve the pain.
3 Seek medical help immediately.

First aid when stung by a beaked sea snake, blue-ringed octopus or marbled cone snail

1 Keep the person calm, reassured and still.
2 Apply firm pressure over the bite or sting area. Use your hand if necessary.

3 Using firm pressure, apply a bandage over the bite or sting area.
4 For a bite on the arm or leg, apply another bandage. Starting near the fingers or toes, firmly bandage upwards, covering as much of the limb as possible. Keep the limb still by using a splint.
5 Seek medical help immediately.
6 Monitor the person and give CPR if needed.

First aid when stung by a box jellyfish

1 As soon as possible, pour domestic vinegar over the sting area for at least 30 seconds.
2 Seek medical help immediately.

First aid when bitten by a shark or crocodile

1 Keep the person calm.
2 Apply pressure to the bite site to stop the bleeding.
3 Cover the person lightly with clothing or a towel.
4 Seek medical help immediately.

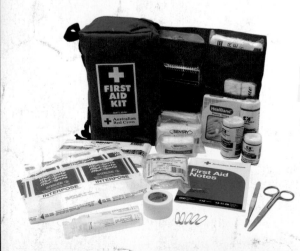

GLOSSARY

aggressive angry and often ready to attack

anti-venom medicine that stops the effect of a poisonous sting or bite

breed produce new baby animals

camouflage spots, stripes, other patterns or colours on an animal that allow it to blend in with its environment

coelenterates invertebrates that are soft bodied and do not have a hard, protective outer layer

crustaceans marine animals that have a hard, protective outer layer, such as lobsters and prawns

ecosystem a collection of plants, animals and other living things that live together in the same environment and rely on each other in order to live

endangered in danger of becoming extinct

estuaries the wide part of a river close to where it meets the sea, which contains a mix of fresh and salt water

extinct wiped out, or no longer alive anywhere on Earth

extinction becoming extinct – wiped out, or no longer alive anywhere on Earth

food chain a linked system of animals, plants and other living things in which each member is eaten in turn by another member

habitats environments where animals and plants live

invertebrates animals without backbones

molluscs animals with soft bodies that are usually protected by a shell, such as snails

nocturnal active (usually hunting) at night

overfishing when large numbers of fish are caught and not enough fish are left in the ocean

paralysed made so that the body is unable to move

predators meat-eating animals that hunt, kill and eat other animals

proboscis a kind of long snout growing from the head of an animal

reefs sections of rock or coral just below the surface of the ocean, usually close to the shore

species a group of animals or other living things that share similar features and behaviours

temperate from the mild climate region between the tropical and polar regions

tropical from the warm climate region around the middle of Earth, near the equator

venom a poisonous or harmful substance produced by an animal, which is injected by a bite or a sting

venomous containing harmful poison, called venom

vertebrates animals with backbones

whaling hunting and killing whales for their oil, meat or bones

INDEX